T0367964

Welcome to the Garden

Welcome to the Garden

Diary of the broken-hearted

Kelsy Lynne

ARCHWAY
PUBLISHING

Archway Publishing books may be ordered through booksellers or by contacting:

Archway Publishing
1663 Liberty Drive
Bloomington, IN 47403
www.archwaypublishing.com
844-669-3957

Because of the dynamic nature of the Internet, any web addresses or
links contained in this book may have changed since publication and
may no longer be valid. The views expressed in this work are solely those
of the author and do not necessarily reflect the views of the publisher,
and the publisher hereby disclaims any responsibility for them.

Any people depicted in stock imagery provided by Getty Images are
models, and such images are being used for illustrative purposes only.
Certain stock imagery © Getty Images.

ISBN: 978-1-6657-6101-7 (sc)
ISBN: 978-1-6657-6102-4 (hc)
ISBN: 978-1-6657-6103-1 (e)

Library of Congress Control Number: 2024911583

Print information available on the last page.

Archway Publishing rev. date: 06/13/2024

Contents

Immoral Rose

It all started with a wooden rose-
Easy enough to open yet too fragile to close,
How intriguing it was, the knowing that wood can never die-
Materialistic things keeping me at an all-time high,
It may never die but it will never bloom-
That is factual; something I can presume.

Refuge

They used what I gave, held it to their standard of power-
Every apology, miscommunication killing me tender,
I was everything sweet, in a world full of such sour-
Using the depth of my soul to an advantage, I'd then surrender.

Inflicted Nightmare

I was like paradise,
Selflessly giving you a taste-
Yet even in my dreams,
You took and took, letting me go to waste.

Justification

I made excuses for them until I was blue in the face-
Each "who," "where," and "why" ended in such disgrace,
I made excuses for every lie I fell into-
I was selfish and clueless to everything see-through,
I made excuses each time I'd begin to walk away-
Based off of the best words used to get me to stay.

Neutral

There was not one thing that could compare-
The magic, the silence, the tears behind each stare,
I was unfadable but solemnly incapable-
Keeping me close and calling me irreplaceable,
Selfless, gentle, yet deathly insane-
Helpless, uneasy, and full of such pain.

Pearl Necklace

Tolerated everything, down to the last conversation-
Waiting on them hand and foot, making me a desperation,
The ringing in my ears, becoming my own downfall-
Perfectly imperfected, a professional in letting them have me raw,
All I wanted to hear, the things keeping me at an all-time high-
Yet, even when they were honest, it was somehow a lie.

The Following

I went down into your gutter-
Keeping myself hidden inside of your head,
I organized your heart full of clutter-
Time-and-time again to keep your pride overfed.

Convenient

Contaminated with horrific pain, you knew it best-
Pushed yourself into my life, knowing I was in distress,
Of your choosing, holding me in your arms-
Leading me to be comfortable, far away from harm,
Trying to comprehend me, acting on my flawed forms-
Convincing me in my own head, setting silence to my storms.

Take me Home

Persistently talking up my head-
Insisting that I wouldn't be misled,
No appetite, no exhaustion, I just watch you function well-
Watching it all happen before me, living in someone else's Hell,
Too many promises, all your words; the physical apologies-
Saying all that I needed, merely based on psychology.

Tricking me Numb

Saying I'm yours, making me need you-
Making yourself a lie then breaking me in two,
Abandoned, shattered, feeling the resentment of such pretend-
Most of all, left with the scars that will never have an end,

Watering my Flowers

The devotion to such intimacy,
Aching at the bones-
Causing the Devil to act innocently,
Faced with such unknown-
Shaking through infatuation,
Each word slurring off the tongue-
The presence, becoming a fixation,
But absent, puncturing each lung.

Til Death

Loading the ammunition,
Preparing for the war,
Holding the position,
One that's not deserved anymore-
Praying for such mercy,
An acceptance to each scheme-
Fighting until the death,
Reaching such an extreme.

You and I

Being more than just a feeling,
Instead, a connection out of our reach-
Deeper than two souls touching,
Deeper than what we're able to teach-
This quench is not harmless,
It's a hunger that must be fed-
Without it we are not living,
But who's to say that we aren't dead?

Robotic

Devaluing me when I needed them most-
Loving me than turning into a ghost,
Distance between us simply growing in size-
The truths they'd tell include subconscious lies,
Such silence, chosen of their selection-
Being the trial-run to their newest invention.

Tale of the Victim

All you want to do is help them change-
You will lose yourself trying to help what is out of your range,
You will attempt to save what is lost-
You will not realize all that it will cost,
Do not forget about all of the energy gone wasted-
Do not forget all of the tears and how they tasted.

Echo

It was easy to resent,
I did so with a grin-
The time that I spent,
Enduring their sin-
Totality of the ache,
My heart at a pause-
Laws that I'd break,
Them being the cause.

Day by Day

I have long since learnt-
How love should be,
Because you, you burnt-
Those bridges for me,
Yet I'll never forget-
That exact taste,
Each tear put me in debt-
Each tear went to waste,
I finally had the courage,
I finally had the heart,
I chose myself,
I built me back together part-by-part.

I Do

I wish for your soul to always be fed-
I pray you to Heaven before you are dead,
I say it now as I said it then-
This kind of love does not have an end.

Jaded

May you find the comfort, in every empty space-
Because you'll never find another, another saving grace.
This is a kind of beautiful that you will not forget,
A fire that never dies, a fire that I set.

Gentle or Not

Praying for me while the sun comes to a set,
Wanting what you can't have, wishing what you can't get-
Being so consistent; they get what they want,
Say all they can say, it all being a common front-
Send me flowers, call my phone,
Each argument resulting in me alone-
Getting what you want and then crossing a line,
Apologies and excuses only lasting for a time.

Justifying Woman

Increasingly picking apart the weaker man,
Feeding your humiliation, entertaining your every fan-
Everything caused after each and every plan made,
The suffering my heart felt to go through such shade-
Led me to love you and then this is what you pull,
Because every heartbroken woman, everyone is a fool.

Wishing for Words

There's a brutal storm going on inside of my head,
While flowers need water to grow, they're being overfed-
I try to follow the rainbow and understand where it has led,
But I get stuck within the storm-
Reading into all that has not been said.

Heart of the Ocean

The stories that we wish for, in this world of sin-
The stories that cut deep, deep into the skin,
The hearts that stayed together, the hearts that died as one-
A love that sunk to the bottom of the ocean; a love never undone,
The love that makes us cry, the love that makes us sick-
Even If given the choice, this love is what we pick.

Despising me Sad

Racing towards me through the fire,
Watching as I slowly burn-
Becoming my hearts every desire,
One that not even I can unlearn-
Playing my part in your fantasy,
Living the unbalanced role-
The worsening of my insanity,
As the words and promises take such a toll.

Ready? Go!

You won't escape this fight,
A mission that cannot be won,
You are a prisoner to your own army,
Unable to undo what has been done.

Desired Apologies

Drowning in the feelings you cannot see-
Running circles around a grieving spree,
Battling a demon that won't set you free-
Constantly looking for a golden key.

Where we Left off

It's as if I don't know you, but I've been here before,
Letting many selfish people walk through my door-
The words that I'd lean on, the feelings I'd exchange,
The commitments I'd been promised, so quick to change.

Dedicated

It's almost as if every you, every you knows me best,
But every you that I meet, they're just like the rest-
Every time is new, but every time becomes similar,
Every memory before what's new, just becomes a blur-
I was told it must get worse before it gets better,
It's you that told me that, but we can't kill the messenger.

Loving to the Bone

My hands shake, my arms can no longer pull-
My heart begins to ache as I run low on fuel,
I'm dizzy behind the eyes, blind with such thought-
Reminiscing on it all, all I was once taught,
The bones become weak; the tears begin to shed-
Bones are now breaking, breaking over words they were once fed.

Limited Edition

You called me an object, a creation within your mind,
Forming me to be what you want, a personal design-
My arms on strings, you'd move them as you please,
This kind of puppetry is known as a disease.

Being Taught

There are beautiful stories behind the words that I write-
There is so much darkness behind my radiance of light,
I could write anything off the emotions that I feel-
Becoming so lost in my stories, as they seem too surreal.

Deserving

I will always be in the back of your mind,
A love like mine, you will seek to find-
In a world like this, someone might take my place,
But a world like this, my love cannot be replaced-
Without knowing, my heart is what you will serve,
Now you know, it's what you deserve.

Anguished

I was selflessly generous-
And you knew it all too well,
You took until I had less-and-less-
My heart was yours to sell,
I betrayed my own peace-
Watched you push me to the side,
You found a desperate release-
While I questioned why you lied,
You burned me in all the right places-
I watched but could not see,
You ended up having many different faces-
Each one taking the worst toll on me.

Do Remember

I forgive you for each scar-
As the tears stream down my face,
I forgive you from afar-
This, you cannot ever replace.

Meeting for Two

It is the aftermath that will hurt the most,
They welcomed you into their Hell, they were your host-
Avoid the bruising, collect the scars, stray away from this disease,
You are not their cure; you've become their tease.

See you soon

I think of you often and all we could've been-
I now forgive you, for each and every sin,
I loved you at your worst and I always will-
I'll be in love with you forever even if time stands still,
I will always smile when I think of you and me-
I will always be yours, unconditionally.

Amongst Us

The petals stay still, they'll never fall-
No thorns to prick, no thorns at all,
Silent in smell, having no scent-
Living forever as self-torment.

Silent Night

I made excuses for the tears, belittling my fears-
All to end up feeding your pride, for so many years,
I love you but I love you not-
Most of all I hate you for letting me rot.

Repair

For you cannot tell,
The things that go on in my mind-
From Heaven I fell,
Where I was taught to be kind-
Yet there are voids within me,
Those that one simply cannot fill-
There is damage you cannot see,
Damage that makes the world stand still.

June Game

Breaking each barrier, overcoming the walls I built-
Despising the wall I let down when you left without guilt.
So, tell me, tell me please what's the use?
I am the victim to your sequence of abuse.
You were delicate, charming, so easy with me-
Acting like everything that I needed, remarkably.

'Fond of the Yous'

When my mind is clear, is it always just you?
Or is my heart relapsing and unable to pull through?
It's gotten so deep, there's a you in every place,
Every look that's different still only shows your face-
Shame on the yous' for taking me out of my mind,
But shame on me, I let the yous' take my peace of mind.

Skeletons

Difficult to bend my knees, yet, harder to simply walk-
Unable to speak any words; impaired when I talk,
Is this a concussion? Am I going blind?
Or am I breaking, breaking over what's going on in my mind?
Cracking of the bones, minute-by-minute and up to time-
A skeleton I was- A skeleton to confine.

Made for

Just like people, objects can be scratched-
Unlike objects, people become attached,
You may become infatuated with my art-
I warned you, I am only an object, one with an artificial heart.

Welcome to the Carnival

You are knocking on the doors of Hell,
You are so consumed that you can't even tell-
You are hearing what you wish, taking part in your own delusion,
You then blame yourself; you were wrapped in emotional confusion.

First piece

There is a kind of beautiful that you cannot see,
A catastrophe that's cut into sharp parts of three.
The first piece stitches to the core,
While the sharpness of that edge-
Will make you crave more.

Second piece

The second of the three,
Shatters all that aches,
Binding onto you-
Feelings you cannot forsake.

Third piece

The third of all the blades,
It will leave a scar,
You'll relive each moment-
As I watch from afar.

The Tears that Got me Here

There is a poetic grace behind each building that has fell-
There is a beautiful peace within each human labeled unwell-
There is a timeless compassion behind every farewell,
And there is an exquisite detail behind each story that I tell.

Printed in the United States
by Baker & Taylor Publisher Services